Silent Weapon

John Shenton

Published by John Shenton, 2024.

While every precaution has been taken in the preparation of this book, the publisher assumes no responsibility for errors or omissions, or for damages resulting from the use of the information contained herein.

SILENT WEAPON

First edition. September 21, 2024.

Copyright © 2024 John Shenton.

ISBN: 979-8227605931

Written by John Shenton.

Table of Contents

Foreword 1

Chapter 1: China's Historical Approach to Warfare 3

Chapter 2: The Opium Wars: A Precedent for Drug Warfare 11

Chapter 3: The Rise of Synthetic Drugs in China 16

Chapter 4: State-Sponsored Production: The Role of the Chinese Government 21

Chapter 5: Fentanyl as a Tool of Hybrid Warfare 26

Chapter 6: Cartel Connections: The Role of Mexico in Fentanyl Trafficking 31

Chapter 7: The Southern U.S. Border: A Weak Link in the Fight Against Fentanyl 36

Chapter 8: The Human Cost: Fentanyl's Devastation in the United States 42

Chapter 9: Weaknesses in U.S. Law and Enforcement Responses . 47

Chapter 10: Reclassifying Fentanyl Trafficking as Murderous Intent 52

Chapter 11: Labeling Cartels as Terrorist Organizations 57

Chapter 12: Future Strategies for Combating the Fentanyl Crisis 63

Chapter 13: The Endgame – The Looming Shadow of Open Conflict 69

Epilogue: A War Yet to End 73

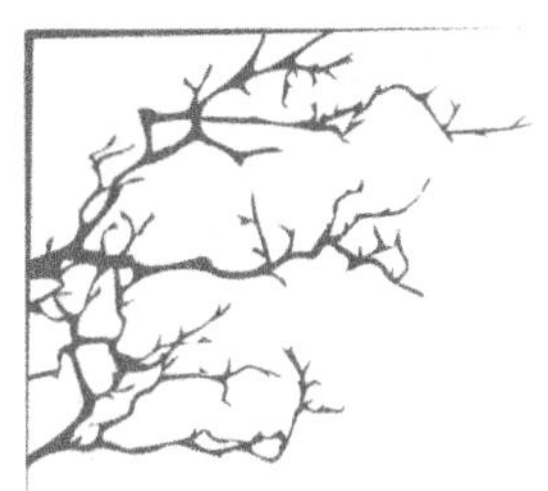

Foreword

The 21st century has ushered in a new era of warfare that transcends traditional battlegrounds of bullets and bombs and instead seeps into the very fabric of societies. As the lines between war and peace blur, nations engage in hybrid warfare employing economic, cyber, and psychological strategies to undermine their adversaries from within. In this context, a chilling reality has emerged: the opioid crisis devastating the United States may not be a mere consequence of the global drug trade, but a calculated assault orchestrated by foreign powers. At the heart of this silent war is China, with its potent weapon fentanyl.

The synthetic opioid fentanyl is far more than just a drug. It is a strategic tool, one that has claimed thousands of lives, ravaged communities, and overwhelmed the U.S. healthcare and law enforcement systems. As overdose rates soar, the question must be asked: Is this epidemic an unintended by-product of globalization, or something more sinister?

This book, *The Silent Weapon: China's Fentanyl War Against the West*, is an exploration of the grim possibility that fentanyl is being used as a deliberate tactic in China's ongoing hybrid warfare against the United States. With precision and insight, the chapters ahead trace China's long history of unconventional warfare, from the Warring States period to the lessons learned during the Opium Wars, drawing eerie parallels between the past and present. By delving into China's role as the world's leading producer of fentanyl precursors, and its connections to Mexican drug cartels, this book uncovers the dark web of international networks driving the current opioid crisis.

But this book is not merely a historical or geopolitical treatise. It is a call to action. The consequences of this modern war seen in the form of overdoses, addiction, and societal decay are felt daily in American homes. Through meticulous research, the author shines a light on the failures of U.S. law enforcement, border security, and diplomatic efforts that have allowed this crisis to fester. More importantly, the book offers bold solutions, advocating for reclassifying fentanyl distribution as an act of murderous intent and proposing the designation of Mexican cartels as terrorist organizations.

In an age where the battlefield has shifted, this work serves as both a wake-up call and a roadmap for reclaiming control. It compels readers to recognize that the fight against fentanyl is not just a public health emergency, but a national security imperative.

As you read the pages ahead, you will be confronted with the unsettling truth of how a single drug has been weaponized to wreak havoc on the United States. But you will also be empowered with knowledge—knowledge that can drive the policy changes, enforcement strategies, and international cooperation necessary to turn the tide in this silent war.

This is a battle we cannot afford to lose.

John Shenton

Chapter 1: China's Historical Approach to Warfare

The Chinese philosophy of warfare has evolved over millennia, rooted in a deep understanding of strategy, pragmatism, and the necessity for adaptability in the face of changing threats. Unlike many civilizations that approached conflict with an emphasis on brute force or decisive, climactic battles, China's strategic culture has historically favoured subtlety, patience, and the indirect route to victory. From the Warring States period (475-221 BC) through to modern times, this approach has underscored a unique blend of military, political, economic, and psychological tactics—allowing China to outmanoeuvre stronger adversaries without the need for confrontation.

The Warring States Period: A School of Strategic Thought

China's Warring States period (475-221 BC) was a time of intense military and political conflict, as various regional states vied for supremacy over a fractured land. It was during this era that many of China's most profound philosophies on warfare and governance emerged, driven by a need for survival in an environment of constant threat. The competition between the states fostered the development of new tactics, technologies, and theories on how best to wage war, but it also encouraged a broader view of conflict itself.

The most enduring legacy from this period is *The Art of War*, attributed to Sun Tzu. This seminal work on strategy is a masterpiece of subtlety, with its teachings focused on indirect warfare, psychological manipulation, and the maximization of advantage while minimizing confrontation. Sun Tzu advocated for avoiding conflict unless necessary, urging leaders to instead weaken their enemies through division, deception, and the exploitation of their weaknesses.

Sun Tzu's famous tenet that "the supreme art of war is to subdue the enemy without fighting" captures the essence of Chinese military thought during this period. The emphasis on strategy over brute force is evident in the countless power struggles of the Warring States, where smaller, less powerful states often survived through alliances, diplomacy, or the strategic manipulation of their neighbours' vulnerabilities. This foundational idea of winning without direct combat laid the groundwork for China's future approaches to warfare, transcending the battlefield and permeating other spheres of influence.

The Evolution of Unconventional Tactics

Sun Tzu's strategies were only the beginning of China's long-standing preference for unconventional warfare. Throughout its imperial history, China demonstrated a profound ability to use non-military means to achieve military ends. From economic sanctions and resource manipulation to the use of spies and misinformation, China often sought to create conditions that would weaken its enemies before a sword was ever drawn.

This indirect approach was evident in China's handling of foreign threats as well. For instance, during the Tang dynasty (618-907 AD), China frequently dealt with nomadic tribes along its borders not by engaging them directly but by fostering internal divisions among rival groups, strategically cutting off supply routes, or offering gifts and trade deals that kept potential threats preoccupied or beholden to Chinese influence. This "divide and conquer" approach allowed China to maintain control over its periphery without the costs of constant warfare, reinforcing the idea that conflict could be managed through diplomacy, economic pressure, and psychological tactics.

The Ming dynasty (1368-1644) offers further examples of unconventional strategies. When faced with the threat of Mongol resurgence, the Ming leadership constructed the Great Wall to deter incursions but simultaneously used diplomacy to foster alliances with Mongol tribes and other Central Asian powers. The Ming rulers understood that raw military might alone would not be sufficient to secure their borders, so they deployed a blend of defensive architecture, psychological deterrence, and strategic alliances.

Psychological Warfare: The Mind as the Battlefield

Chinese military thought has always placed significant importance on the psychological aspects of warfare. The objective is not simply to defeat the enemy on the battlefield but to break their will to fight, sow discord, and create conditions where the opponent's defeat is inevitable without confrontation. This has been a hallmark of Chinese strategy throughout history, and it is epitomized in Sun Tzu's teachings on deception and the importance of morale.

In the Three Kingdoms period (220-280 AD), one

of China's most famous military tacticians, Zhuge Liang, consistently employed psychological warfare to outwit his enemies. In the battle of Red Cliffs (208 AD), for example, Zhuge famously used misinformation and environmental manipulation to deceive a much larger force, leading to a stunning victory with minimal loss of life. His reliance on cunning, timing, and an understanding of human nature showcased the depth of China's approach to warfare, where the battlefield was not only a physical space but also a theatre for psychological contest.

The importance of morale and psychological strength has long been a central theme in Chinese warfare, where demoralizing the enemy often took precedence over direct conflict. Chinese commanders were known to exploit fear, uncertainty, and division within enemy ranks to weaken their resolve, making them easier to defeat. The famous "empty fort strategy" from *The Thirty-Six Stratagems* collection, where an undefended position is used to bluff an attacking force into retreat, epitomizes this approach.

The Modern Extension: Hybrid Warfare

In modern times, China's historical approach to warfare has adapted to contemporary challenges, yet the underlying principles remain the same. The concept of "hybrid warfare" a blend of conventional and unconventional methods, including cyberattacks, economic coercion, and psychological operations aligns closely with China's long-standing strategic philosophy.

Economic manipulation has been a central tool in China's modern hybrid warfare. Through control of critical supply chains, strategic investments in foreign infrastructure, and the leveraging of debt, China has extended its influence globally without resorting to military force. This economic statecraft is a direct descendant of Sun Tzu's teachings, wherein weakening an opponent's economy can be as effective, if not more so, than attacking their armies.

Additionally, China's extensive use of information warfare, particularly in the digital age, mirrors the psychological tactics of past eras. By spreading disinformation, conducting cyber espionage, and utilizing soft power through media and cultural influence, China continues to wage a form of psychological warfare aimed at shaping perceptions, undermining adversaries, and securing its strategic objectives.

The Modern Drug Crisis: An Extension of Philosophy?

One area where these tactics may manifest is in the global drug crisis. Some analysts argue that China's approach to the production and distribution of synthetic opioids like fentanyl reflects a broader strategy of weakening opponents through internal destabilization. This can be viewed as a modern adaptation of China's age-old philosophy of indirect warfare, where rather than confronting an adversary on the battlefield, a nation might instead exploit its societal weaknesses.

The opioid epidemic has severely strained Western nations, particularly the United States, contributing to a decline in public health, increasing crime rates, and creating significant economic and social burdens. Whether deliberate or a consequence of global markets, the influx of drugs into foreign nations bears a striking resemblance to the historical Chinese tactic of weakening enemies from within targeting the internal cohesion of a society rather than its military strength.

Conclusion: A Timeless Strategy

China's historical approach to warfare, from the Warring States period to the present day, reveals a consistent preference for indirect, strategic, and unconventional means of defeating enemies. From Sun Tzu's *The Art of War* to modern hybrid

tactics, China has sought to outmanoeuvre, outthink, and outlast its adversaries by exploiting their weaknesses rather than confronting them head-on. Whether through psychological warfare, economic manipulation, or the fostering of internal divisions, China's strategy has remained one of subtlety and patience, a testament to the enduring influence of its ancient philosophies on modern geopolitics.

As we explore the implications of these strategies in contemporary conflicts, we see that China's long game continues to shape its approach to warfare—one that emphasizes weakening opponents through means that go beyond the battlefield. Understanding this history is crucial to comprehending the full scope of China's global ambitions today.

Chapter 2: The Opium Wars: A Precedent for Drug Warfare

The Opium Wars of the 19th century stand as a stark reminder of how narcotics can be weaponized, not just against individuals but against entire nations. These conflicts, fought between China and Western powers—most notably the British Empire—over the importation and trade of opium, significantly altered the trajectory of Chinese history. The wars laid bare the devastating effects of addiction, economic manipulation, and the ruthless exercise of imperial power. Two centuries later, the echoes of this conflict resonate in what some perceive as a reversal of roles, with China now accused of weaponizing another potent opioid, fentanyl, against the West, particularly the United States.

The Opium Wars: A Nation's Descent into Addiction

The Opium Wars were fought in two phases: The First Opium War (1839-1842) and the Second Opium War (1856-1860). These wars emerged from a deep conflict of interest between the Qing Dynasty and Western imperial powers, particularly Britain. By the early 19th century, China had a robust internal economy and was self-sufficient, exporting tea, silk, and porcelain to Europe in exchange for silver. However, the West had little that China desired in return, and this trade imbalance deeply troubled the British.

Britain's solution was to exploit a growing Chinese demand for opium, a product they could supply in abundance from their colonies in India. By flooding China with opium, the British reversed the trade imbalance, drawing silver out of the Chinese economy and simultaneously addicting millions of Chinese citizens. The Qing government, recognizing the social and economic devastation caused by the opium epidemic, attempted to prohibit its import. This culminated in the Opium Wars, as Britain, seeking to protect its lucrative trade, resorted to military force to compel China to continue the drug's acceptance.

The wars had profound consequences. Militarily, China was outmatched and humiliated, forced to cede Hong Kong to Britain and grant extraterritorial rights to foreign powers. Economically, the outflow of silver devastated the Chinese economy, and socially, the nation grappled with the deep scars left by widespread addiction. China was plunged into what is often termed its "Century of Humiliation," a period characterized by foreign domination and internal strife.

Fentanyl Crisis: A Modern Reversal

Today, the United States and much of the West find themselves entangled in an opioid crisis of their own, with fentanyl at its heart. Fentanyl, a synthetic opioid far more potent than heroin or morphine, has flooded U.S. streets, contributing to a staggering number of overdose deaths each year. According to many reports, much of this fentanyl or its precursor chemicals are manufactured in China, often in clandestine labs, before being trafficked through global supply chains. This phenomenon raises a striking parallel to the Opium Wars, with many now viewing China not as the victim of the narcotics trade, but as its manipulator.

While the comparison between the Opium Wars and today's fentanyl crisis is not exact, the similarities are unsettling. Both crises involve foreign powers leveraging narcotics to destabilize a rival nation, both have had catastrophic social impacts, and both reveal the vulnerabilities inherent in global trade systems. The historical irony, that China—a nation that once suffered deeply from the influx of foreign opium—is now a major source of the precursor chemicals fueling the U.S. opioid epidemic, is unmistakable.

Economic and Societal Impacts

The economic effects of the Opium Wars were disastrous for China. The influx of opium not only drained the economy of silver but also weakened the productivity of the Chinese populace, many of whom succumbed to addiction. As addiction rates soared, so too did social unrest, corruption, and inefficiency within the Qing administration. Entire regions of the empire became riddled with despair, further eroding the power of the central government.

Similarly, the economic effects of the modern fentanyl crisis on the United States are severe. While the economic losses may not be as immediately visible as the depletion of silver reserves in Qing China, they are nonetheless vast. The U.S. spends billions each year on healthcare, law enforcement, and rehabilitation programs to combat the opioid epidemic. Families and communities are torn apart, leading to long-term economic instability in affected areas, particularly in the rust belt and rural America, where addiction rates have soared.

On a societal level, both drug crises have acted as catalysts for profound cultural and social breakdowns. In Qing China, opium addiction tore through the fabric of traditional Chinese society, leaving a weakened and disoriented population that was easy prey for foreign manipulation. Today, fentanyl has had similarly devastating effects, contributing to a rise in overdose deaths, broken families, and increased crime rates. Much like opium, fentanyl preys on the most vulnerable, exacerbating existing social inequalities and eroding the resilience of communities.

Political Manipulation: Then and Now

Politically, the Opium Wars established a clear precedent for how drugs could be used to assert dominance over a rival nation. Britain's flooding of the Chinese market with opium was a deliberate act of economic and political warfare. The British sought not just to balance trade but to weaken China, to create a more pliable and dependent state that could be easily manipulated. The eventual defeat of China and the resulting "unequal treaties" ensured Western dominance over key Chinese ports and trade routes for decades.

In the 21st century, while the U.S. and China are not engaged in outright military conflict, the geopolitics of the fentanyl crisis carry echoes of the Opium Wars. Some analysts suggest that China's inability or unwillingness to fully crack down on fentanyl production and exportation reflects a broader strategic aim. By allowing fentanyl to flood American markets, China may be engaging in a form of asymmetrical warfare, subtly undermining the social fabric and public health of its chief geopolitical rival without direct military confrontation. In this sense, the lessons of the Opium Wars may have influenced China's approach: a powerful reminder that economic and social destabilization can be as effective as armed conflict in weakening an adversary.

The Irony of History

The irony is hard to escape. A nation that was once the victim of Western-imposed drug warfare may now be using similar tactics in its geopolitical strategy. While direct comparisons between the 19th-century opium trade and the modern fentanyl crisis are imperfect, the underlying dynamics of narcotics as a tool for economic and social manipulation remain strikingly similar. If the Opium Wars taught China anything, it was that drugs could cripple a nation, hollowing it out from within and that such a strategy can be more devastating than confrontation.

Conclusion: Lessons from the Past

As the fentanyl crisis continues to claim lives across the United States, it is important to reflect on the lessons of the Opium Wars. The weaponization of narcotics, whether deliberate or incidental, has long-lasting effects that go beyond individual addiction and social decay—it has the potential to reshape the global balance of power. In the 19th century, China was on the receiving end of such a strategy, and it took more than a century for the nation to recover from its consequences. Today, as the U.S. grapples with its opioid epidemic, it must reckon with the possibility that it, too, is the target of a slow and insidious form of warfare, one that China learned from its painful past. The echoes of history serve as a stark warning that the geopolitical landscape is always evolving, and the tools of conflict are often more subtle—and more deadly—than guns and bombs.

Chapter 3: The Rise of Synthetic Drugs in China

In the last few decades, China has transformed into a dominant force in the global synthetic drug market, with fentanyl a powerful opioid that has ravaged communities worldwide standing at the heart of this transformation. This chapter explores China's role as a key player in the production of synthetic drugs, analyzing the interplay between its rapidly expanding pharmaceutical industry, government regulations, and the global narcotics trade. By examining the networks of production and export, we will gain insight into how China has developed a sophisticated infrastructure to meet global demand while strategically maintaining plausible deniability.

The Pharmaceutical Revolution

China's ascent as a pharmaceutical giant traces back to the liberalization of its economy in the late 20th century. With a burgeoning industrial base, low labour costs, and relaxed regulatory environments, the country quickly became an attractive hub for drug manufacturing. By the 1990s, China was producing bulk quantities of pharmaceuticals, focusing on raw ingredients for various drugs, often referred to as Active Pharmaceutical Ingredients (APIs).

China's pharmaceutical industry soon became a global powerhouse. Its factories produced high volumes of both legal and illegal drugs, especially synthetic ones like fentanyl. Unlike traditional drugs derived from natural sources like opium or coca plants, synthetic drugs rely on chemicals that can be mass-produced at a fraction of the cost and with far greater potency. This shift towards synthetics offered criminal networks an appealing alternative to older narcotic supply chains.

As the demand for opioids surged, particularly in the United States, China emerged as a critical supplier of fentanyl and its chemical precursors, substances required for its synthesis. Fentanyl, originally developed as a potent analgesic for pain management in the 1960s, is 50 to 100 times more powerful than morphine, making it both a highly effective medical solution and a dangerous drug when misused. As its medical use expanded, so too did its illicit trade.

Fentanyl: A Drug of Destruction

Fentanyl's potency and ease of production soon made it a favourite among drug traffickers. Small quantities could be mixed with other narcotics or sold on the illegal market, yielding enormous profits. By the early 2000s, fentanyl was making its way into illegal drug supplies across the world, often without the end user's knowledge, leading to unprecedented overdose rates.

The role of China in this rapidly expanding crisis cannot be overstated. Fentanyl, unlike drugs like heroin or cocaine, does not rely on agricultural production. Instead, it is synthesized in laboratories, where chemicals can be mixed and refined to produce the final product. This chemical foundation made China already established as a major producer of industrial chemicals and pharmaceutical precursors a natural centre for fentanyl production.

Government Regulations: The Plausible Deniability

China's regulatory framework is a complex mosaic that varies by industry, region, and substance. On paper, the Chinese government has strict controls on narcotics and other illegal drugs. However, the oversight of chemical production has long been lax, especially regarding precursor chemicals, which are legal substances used in a wide array of pharmaceutical and industrial processes. Fentanyl's key precursors such as NPP (N-phenethyl-4-piperidone) and 4-ANPP (4-anilino-Nphenethylpiperidine) can be legally manufactured in China, as they have legitimate uses in pharmaceuticals.

While these chemicals are subject to international control under the UN's Convention on Psychotropic Substances, enforcement in China has historically been inconsistent. This lack of stringent regulation, combined with China's vast industrial base, has allowed for the large-scale production and export of fentanyl precursors. Factories producing these chemicals often operate in legal grey zones, exploiting loopholes in both national and international laws. Furthermore, some manufacturers will disguise fentanyl precursors as benign chemicals in shipping manifests, allowing them to evade customs checks in importing countries.

The Chinese government has at times responded to international pressure by tightening regulations on fentanyl production and exports. In 2019, China classified all fentanyl-related substances as controlled, making their unauthorized production and sale illegal. However, the complexity of China's industrial system, coupled with the lucrative nature of the trade, means that enforcement remains uneven. Corruption, local protectionism, and the sheer size of China's chemical industry create significant challenges for regulators.

This has allowed Chinese manufacturers to continue producing and exporting fentanyl precursors, often with the appearance of compliance. By exporting the precursors rather than the final product, China shifts the burden of illegal fentanyl production to other countries, particularly Mexico, where cartels complete the synthesis and smuggle the drug into the United States.

Key Regions and Networks

Fentanyl and its precursors are primarily produced in China's eastern and southern provinces, where the country's industrial heartland is located. Provinces like Jiangsu, Guangdong, and Zhejiang have become hubs for chemical and pharmaceutical production. These regions benefit from advanced infrastructure, easy access to ports, and established manufacturing sectors, making them ideal for both legitimate and illicit production.

In these areas, sprawling networks of chemical manufacturers, brokers, and exporters operate with a degree of autonomy that makes oversight difficult. Some of these companies produce fentanyl precursors knowingly, while others may be unaware of the ultimate use of their products. Exporters work with a range of intermediaries who arrange for the shipment of these chemicals to customers in North America, Europe, and elsewhere.

Online platforms and the dark web have become crucial tools in these networks, allowing buyers and sellers to connect anonymously. Chinese chemical companies, often advertised as legitimate businesses, offer fentanyl precursors for sale to international buyers. Payment is made through untraceable cryptocurrencies, and the chemicals are shipped covertly, disguised as other legal products.

While fentanyl itself has become a focal point, China's production of other synthetic drugs is also significant. Methamphetamines, synthetic cannabinoids, and designer drugs such as "bath salts" have all flowed out of China's chemical factories, further entrenching the country's role in the global synthetic drug trade.

The Global Impact

China's role in the production and distribution of synthetic drugs has had far-reaching consequences. The opioid epidemic in the United States, driven in large part by the flood of fentanyl, has claimed hundreds of thousands of lives. Fentanyl's introduction into drug supplies has made already dangerous narcotics like heroin exponentially more lethal. A single dose can be fatal, and the proliferation of fentanyl-laced drugs has overwhelmed public health systems worldwide.

Beyond the immediate human cost, the rise of synthetic drugs has reshaped global narcotics markets. Traditional drug trafficking routes, which relied on the cultivation of plants and the movement of large shipments of narcotics, are being replaced by chemical supply chains that are harder to track and dismantle. China's role in this transformation has positioned it at the nexus of a new type of drug trade one based on industrial production and chemical expertise.

Conclusion

The rise of synthetic drugs in China, particularly fentanyl, reflects a complex interaction between the country's industrial growth, regulatory environment, and global demand for narcotics. While China's pharmaceutical industry has brought many benefits to the world, it has also inadvertently fueled one of the deadliest drug crises in history. By producing the chemical precursors that feed global fentanyl production, China has become an indispensable link in the chain of synthetic drug manufacturing.

China's ability to maintain plausible deniability in the face of this growing crisis is a testament to the intricate and often opaque nature of its regulatory system. The challenge for the international community is not only to address the global demand for these drugs but also to work with China to close the loopholes that allow this trade to flourish. Without coordinated efforts, the rise of synthetic drugs will continue to devastate communities around the world, with China at the centre of this new global narcotics economy.

Chapter 4: State-Sponsored Production: The Role of the Chinese Government

The rise of fentanyl as a global threat has shone a spotlight on the complex role China plays in its production and distribution. While fentanyl itself is often associated with the devastating opioid crisis in North America, its chemical precursors are sourced from China. These substances, which are integral to the synthesis of fentanyl, are produced under the guise of legitimate pharmaceutical operations. The Chinese government, either through calculated neglect or active support, has become enmeshed in a global supply chain that fuels one of the most destructive illicit drug markets in history.

This chapter will examine how the Chinese government has facilitated or, at the very least, tolerated the production and export of fentanyl precursors. Through a mix of political, economic, and legal frameworks, the government has enabled the growth of these activities, presenting challenges to international efforts to stem the tide of this crisis. We will also explore China's often contradictory position in the global fight against narcotics, where its stated policy of strict drug control conflicts with its role as a leading supplier of chemicals that enable the production of illicit opioids.

Historical Context of Pharmaceutical Production in China

To understand China's role in fentanyl precursor production, it is essential to first appreciate the evolution of its pharmaceutical industry. Over the past several decades, China has emerged as one of the world's largest producers of pharmaceutical chemicals. This rapid growth has been driven by both domestic demand and international export markets, with the government supporting the industry as a key sector in the national economy. Pharmaceutical manufacturers, chemical companies, and scientific research institutions have been incentivized to produce a wide range of chemical compounds, many of which are precursors for both legitimate and illicit drug production.

In parallel, China has developed a highly sophisticated and often opaque regulatory environment that governs chemical production. While this system is designed to ensure the safe and controlled use of chemicals, it has created opportunities for illicit activities to flourish under legal cover. This grey area between legal and illegal production is where fentanyl precursors thrive, shielded by legal ambiguities and lax enforcement.

The Role of Political and Economic Forces

At the heart of China's involvement in the fentanyl precursor trade is a confluence of political and economic factors. On one hand, the Chinese government has strong incentives to support its chemical and pharmaceutical industries. These industries contribute to China's economic growth, particularly through exports to global markets. Encouraging industrial growth, including chemical production, aligns with broader state policy objectives of economic development and maintaining employment in key sectors.

On the other hand, China's regulatory and enforcement framework is frequently undermined by local corruption and regional political dynamics. In some cases, local officials may ignore illicit chemical production or export due to the economic benefits these activities provide to their regions. This decentralized enforcement of national laws means that even when the central government takes steps to regulate or ban certain substances, those efforts are inconsistently applied across the country. This creates a permissive environment for the production and export of fentanyl precursors, particularly in regions with strong industrial bases and local government incentives to protect economic interests.

Legal Mechanisms and Loopholes

From a legal perspective, the production of fentanyl precursors occupies a grey zone in China's regulatory framework. Many of the chemicals used in the synthesis of fentanyl are classified as legal pharmaceutical ingredients, which makes regulating their production and distribution a complex task. The Chinese government has made some efforts to crack down on these substances, placing several fentanyl analogues and precursors on controlled substances lists. However, these efforts have been undermined by loopholes in the law and the ability of chemical producers to modify the chemical structures of their products to stay one step ahead of regulators.

China's pharmaceutical sector operates under a rigorous framework, but enforcement of regulations is inconsistent. While the central government may issue bans or restrictions on certain chemicals, enforcement at the provincial and local levels varies, often due to competing economic interests. In some instances, chemical manufacturers can exploit these gaps by slightly altering the chemical composition of their products, thereby evading regulation. As a result, companies can continue to legally produce and export chemicals that, although technically different from those explicitly banned, serve the same purpose in the illicit fentanyl supply chain.

International Narcotics Control Efforts and China's Role

China's relationship with international narcotics control efforts is fraught with contradictions. On the global stage, China portrays itself as a strong advocate for drug control, participating in international forums such as the United Nations Office on Drugs and Crime (UNODC) and cooperating with foreign governments in drug interdiction efforts. Yet, the country's role as a major supplier of fentanyl precursors undermines these efforts, creating a paradox in its approach to international drug control.

China's participation in international narcotics control treaties is often touted as a sign of its commitment to fighting the global drug trade. However, its domestic enforcement of these commitments leaves much to be desired. While China has made some moves to cooperate with international partners, including the United States, in addressing the fentanyl crisis, these efforts are frequently hampered by bureaucratic inertia, conflicting economic interests, and, at times, an apparent unwillingness to fully clamp down on the problem. This has led to frustration among foreign governments, particularly the U.S., which sees China as both a key player in the global drug crisis and a reluctant partner in efforts to resolve it.

State Policy and Fentanyl Production

China's state policy regarding fentanyl production and export is shaped by its broader economic and geopolitical priorities. The government's desire to maintain economic growth and protect key industries often takes precedence over efforts to regulate chemical production. This tension is reflected in the inconsistent application of drug control laws and the persistent gaps in enforcement that allow fentanyl precursor production to continue.

Moreover, China's foreign policy objectives may also play a role in its handling of the fentanyl crisis. The country's relationship with the United States has been marked by tension and rivalry in recent years. Some analysts have speculated that China's lukewarm response to U.S. pressure on fentanyl precursors may be influenced by broader geopolitical considerations. In this view, China's willingness to address the issue may be contingent on the broader context of U.S.-China relations, particularly in areas such as trade negotiations and diplomatic engagement.

Conclusion

China's role in the production and export of fentanyl precursors is emblematic of the complex interplay between economic, political, and legal forces that shape the country's industrial landscape. While the government has taken some steps to regulate the production of these chemicals, its efforts have been inconsistent, often hampered by local corruption, economic priorities, and regulatory loopholes. Moreover, China's participation in international narcotics control efforts is undermined by its role as a leading supplier of the chemicals that fuel the global fentanyl crisis.

China's involvement in the fentanyl precursor trade reflects deeper tensions within the country's approach to industrial policy, international relations, and drug control. The challenge for the international community, particularly countries like the United States, is to find ways to engage with China in a manner that addresses the root causes of this crisis while navigating the broader complexities of the U.S.-China relationship. Only through sustained diplomatic engagement, coupled with domestic reforms within China, can the global community hope to stem the tide of fentanyl production and its devastating consequences.

Chapter 5: Fentanyl as a Tool of Hybrid Warfare

Hybrid warfare has emerged as a dominant paradigm in contemporary geopolitical struggles. Unlike traditional conflicts defined by military engagements or territorial invasions, hybrid warfare is an amorphous, multifaceted approach that blends military, economic, political, cyber, and psychological tactics to achieve strategic objectives. In this chapter, we explore a provocative and increasingly compelling hypothesis: that the export of fentanyl from China to the United States is not merely a by-product of global trade, but part of a broader, deliberate strategy aimed at weakening America's societal and institutional resilience.

Fentanyl, a synthetic opioid significantly more potent than heroin or morphine, has become a focal point of the opioid crisis in the United States. The substance is manufactured in China, although some production has shifted to Mexico in recent years. Its arrival in the U.S. market has been devastating, contributing to over 100,000 overdose deaths in 2023 alone. From a perspective of hybrid warfare, this crisis presents an opportunity to examine how drug addiction, overdose deaths, and societal destabilization could fit into China's broader geopolitical goals.

Fentanyl and the Hybrid Warfare Framework

Hybrid warfare operates on the premise of achieving strategic advantages without engaging in open hostilities. It exploits vulnerabilities within an adversary's societal, economic, and political fabric. A crucial component of hybrid warfare is the utilization of asymmetrical strategies, designed to impose significant harm with minimal risk of confrontation. In this context, the export of fentanyl can be interpreted as a tool used to undermine and destabilize U.S. societal structures.

China, as an emerging global power, has employed various methods to expand its influence while weakening potential adversaries. Much of this strategy has been economic, such as through its Belt and Road Initiative, but it also includes psychological and subversive elements. By allowing the mass export of fentanyl precursors, Chinese criminal networks fuel a public health crisis that overwhelms U.S. institutions. This is where fentanyl fits into the concept of hybrid warfare: it exploits the inherent vulnerabilities of American society—particularly its healthcare, law enforcement, and community cohesion.

Targeting Healthcare and Law Enforcement Systems

One of the key objectives of hybrid warfare is to strain the opponent's critical infrastructures. In the case of fentanyl, the U.S. healthcare system is pushed to its limits by the rising number of overdose cases. Hospitals and emergency services are inundated with overdose victims, many of whom require extensive and costly care. The opioid crisis places an unsustainable burden on public health resources, which are already stretched by the rising costs of chronic illnesses and an ageing population.

Simultaneously, law enforcement agencies find themselves grappling with an unprecedented rise in drug-related crimes, smuggling, and distribution networks. The allocation of resources to fight the opioid epidemic diverts attention away from other critical areas such as counterterrorism, cyber threats, and border security. This creates a ripple effect, where local and federal agencies struggle to maintain order, further exacerbating societal instability.

In the broader framework of hybrid warfare, this strategy is remarkably effective. It erodes the opponent's ability to respond to multiple crises simultaneously. With health care systems strained and law enforcement overwhelmed, societal resilience begins to crumble. The long-term effects of a destabilized population fueled by addiction, poverty, and crime may extend to economic instability and declining trust in institutions, both of which can degrade national unity and resolve.

The Societal Impact: Destabilization from Within

Fentanyl's role in destabilizing society is evident in its destructive social effects. Drug addiction, especially at the scale seen in the opioid epidemic, weakens family structures, erodes community cohesion, and increases crime. Neighborhoods plagued by addiction often suffer from lower property values, higher rates of unemployment, and diminished social services. The breakdown of these fundamental pillars of society leads to a self-reinforcing cycle of decline.

More insidiously, drug addiction promotes feelings of hopelessness, despair, and distrust of the government and its institutions. People trapped in cycles of addiction are less likely to participate in democratic processes such as voting or civic engagement. Communities decimated by overdose deaths may lose faith in their leaders, believing that their government is incapable of protecting them. This deepening divide between the public and the state could serve the strategic objectives of any external actor seeking to weaken America from within.

The societal degradation caused by fentanyl also serves as fertile ground for political extremism. Marginalized and destabilized populations are more susceptible to radical ideologies. This dynamic not only weakens internal cohesion but also creates the potential for violent domestic unrest, further amplifying the chaos and instability hybrid warfare seeks to achieve.

The Role of China: Deliberate Strategy or Unintended Consequence?

The question of whether China is deliberately using fentanyl as a tool of hybrid warfare is complex. On the one hand, Chinese authorities have denied involvement in the trafficking of fentanyl and have, under U.S.

pressure, taken steps to regulate and curtail its production. However, the extent to which these efforts are genuine is debatable, as many Chinese companies continue to exploit legal loopholes and clandestinely supply the precursor chemicals needed for fentanyl production.

From a strategic perspective, allowing the mass export of fentanyl precursors offers China a low-risk, high-reward avenue to undermine American society. It enables China to damage its rivals without engaging in open conflict. The drug crisis shifts attention and resources away from other key areas where the U.S. could counter Chinese influence, such as in trade negotiations, military advancements in the Asia-Pacific, or global economic competition.

Moreover, drug addiction and its consequences align with the broader objectives of hybrid warfare: weakening the internal cohesion of a geopolitical adversary and eroding public trust in government institutions. Whether or not China orchestrated this as a deliberate strategy, the fentanyl epidemic functions in a way that benefits its long-term geopolitical goals.

COVID-19: Accident or By Design?

In the same vein as the fentanyl crisis, COVID-19 has raised questions about its role in China's geopolitical strategy. Was the outbreak of the pandemic an accident, a byproduct of negligence, or something more sinister? While no definitive evidence exists to suggest that COVID-19 was intentionally released, the global chaos that ensued undeniably provided China with an opportunity to exploit weaknesses in other nations, particularly the United States.

The pandemic overwhelmed U.S. healthcare systems devastated the economy and deepened political divisions. At the same time, China managed to recover more quickly from the crisis, at least in terms of its manufacturing and export capacity, and positioned itself as a global leader in pandemic response, particularly in developing nations. The chaos and uncertainty brought by COVID-19 contributed to global instability, much like the opioid epidemic, and played a role in reshaping the international order.

From a hybrid warfare perspective, whether COVID-19 was an accident, or a deliberate act may be less important than the strategic opportunities it afforded China. The destabilization of American society, the erosion of public trust, and the redirection of critical resources away from countering Chinese influence were all outcomes that aligned with China's long-term strategic objectives. Even if COVID-19 was an unintended consequence of a lab leak or wildlife market, the crisis was exploited in ways that served the broader aims of weakening U.S. global leadership.

Conclusion: Hybrid Warfare's New Frontier

Fentanyl and COVID-19 both represent facets of a new type of warfare, one that exploits the soft underbelly of a society's structures. While traditional military power remains a factor in international relations, hybrid warfare increasingly emphasizes indirect tactics that weaken an adversary from within, eroding its capacity to respond effectively. The fentanyl crisis may be seen as part of this broader strategy, contributing to a slow erosion of U.S. societal resilience and institutional strength.

Whether deliberate or incidental, China's role in the fentanyl crisis and the broader destabilization of U.S. society through health crises like COVID-19 fits squarely into the framework of hybrid warfare. As the United States grapples with these challenges, the lessons learned will be crucial for its future ability to respond to the evolving nature of global conflict, where the battlefield is not confined to distant lands, but instead, reaches deep into the heart of the nation's borders, institutions, and people.

Chapter 6: Cartel Connections: The Role of Mexico in Fentanyl Trafficking

Fentanyl, a synthetic opioid fifty to a hundred times more potent than morphine, has become a focal point in the global opioid crisis, particularly in the United States. At the heart of this devastating epidemic is a complex international network that links Chinese chemical manufacturers with Mexico's powerful drug cartels, forming a supply chain that moves from the factories of Asia to the streets of North America. This chapter delves into the collaboration between these disparate entities, examining how the trafficking of fentanyl is facilitated by an intricate system of political and criminal neglect, corruption, and global commerce.

Chinese Chemical Manufacturers and the Supply of Precursors

At the centre of fentanyl's production is China, where a substantial percentage of the chemicals used to manufacture fentanyl are produced. These precursors, chemical compounds that are legal in many jurisdictions due to their industrial applications, are often sold under the guise of legitimate use. However, a huge portion of these chemicals is funnelled into the illicit drug market, eventually ending up in the hands of Mexico's drug cartels. Chinese companies, often operating in a grey zone of legality, are involved in the production and shipment of these substances.

Despite international pressure, the Chinese government has shown a pattern of reluctance or tacit compliance in cracking down on the production and export of fentanyl precursors. While Beijing has made official commitments to regulate synthetic opioids, enforcement remains inconsistent. The opacity of Chinese bureaucratic systems allows chemical companies to exploit regulatory loopholes, selling vast quantities of chemical precursors to Mexican buyers without scrutiny. In some cases, it is suspected that Chinese officials ignore these exports due to corruption or political convenience, balancing international diplomatic commitments with the internal pressures of maintaining business interests.

The Mexican Cartel Nexus: Sinaloa and Jalisco New Generation Cartels

Once the chemical precursors arrive in Mexico, they are handled by two of the country's most notorious criminal organizations the Sinaloa Cartel and the Jalisco New Generation Cartel (CJNG). These cartels, well-established in the international drug trade, have adapted swiftly to the opportunities presented by fentanyl. Known primarily for their roles in the cocaine and heroin trade, these cartels have expanded into synthetic drugs, drawn by fentanyl's profitability and ease of production.

Processing fentanyl in clandestine laboratories within Mexico's remote regions, the cartels can manufacture enormous quantities of the drug at a low cost. Unlike traditional drugs such as heroin or cocaine, which rely on labour-intensive cultivation and processing, fentanyl can be synthesized quickly and with fewer resources, making it an appealing venture for cartels seeking high returns with reduced operational risks. These labs, often hidden deep within cartel-controlled territories, operate with impunity due to the weak enforcement of Mexico's anti-drug laws and the pervasive corruption that plagues local law enforcement.

The Sinaloa Cartel, historically the largest and most powerful drug-trafficking organization in Mexico, was quick to recognize fentanyl's market potential. Operating under the leadership of figures like Joaquín "El Chapo" Guzmán before his capture, the Sinaloa Cartel has built a vast smuggling network that ensures steady supply routes from Mexico into the United States. The Jalisco New Generation Cartel, a more violent and rapidly expanding competitor, has also entrenched itself in the fentanyl trade, vying for control of key territories and distribution channels. These two organizations dominate the production and export of fentanyl, accounting for much of the drug flowing into the U.S.

The Smuggling Process: From Mexico to the U.S. and Beyond

Smuggling fentanyl across the U.S.-Mexico border has proven to be an efficient and effective operation for the cartels. Unlike bulkier drugs such as cocaine or marijuana, fentanyl's potency allows for smaller, more easily concealed quantities to be trafficked, reducing the risks associated with interception by law enforcement. A few milligrams of fentanyl can deliver hundreds of doses, making it possible for cartels to ship large volumes of the drug in small packages, including inside everyday items like vehicles, food shipments, and clothing.

A massive portion of fentanyl enters the U.S. through legal ports of entry, hidden within the massive volume of legitimate trade that crosses the border daily. The cartels employ sophisticated smuggling techniques, using corrupt officials, advanced technology, and "mules" (individuals paid to carry the drugs across the border) to outmanoeuvre border security. Meanwhile, smaller quantities of fentanyl are sent directly via mail or courier services, often ordered through dark web markets, making detection even more challenging.

Once inside the United States, the distribution network activates, with fentanyl being diluted and mixed with other substances like heroin, cocaine, or even counterfeit prescription pills. This adulteration increases the risk to users, as they often unknowingly consume lethal doses of the drug. From urban centres to rural communities, fentanyl floods the illicit drug market, leading to a catastrophic rise in overdose deaths across the country.

The Role of Mexican and Chinese Governments: A Delicate Balance

Both the Mexican and Chinese governments play complex roles in the fentanyl trade, marked by a combination of enforcement and complicity. In Mexico, the federal government has struggled to effectively combat the cartels' dominance. Despite international cooperation efforts with U.S. law enforcement, the sheer power of cartels in certain regions, coupled with deep-seated corruption, renders many of these initiatives ineffective. Cartels often have major influence over local politicians, police forces, and military personnel, ensuring that their fentanyl operations continue with minimal interference. In regions like Sinaloa and Jalisco, these criminal organizations act as shadow governments, dictating law and order on their terms.

In China, the government's response has been a balancing act. On the one hand, Beijing faces pressure from the U.S. and the international community to clamp down on the production and export of fentanyl precursors. On the other hand, cracking down too harshly on this industry would disrupt a lucrative business sector and potentially anger powerful business interests. Additionally, China's government has little incentive to invest heavily in a problem perceived as being primarily an American issue. The result is a half-hearted effort to regulate fentanyl production, with enforcement ebbing and flowing based on diplomatic pressure rather than sustained domestic policy.

The lack of meaningful collaboration between the two countries, compounded by their internal challenges, has allowed the fentanyl trade to thrive. This mutual reluctance to address the problem head-on contributes to the resilience of the trafficking networks and the continued devastation wrought by fentanyl on populations around the globe.

Conclusion: The Growing Global Threat

The connection between Chinese chemical manufacturers and Mexican cartels represents a potent alliance, one that drives the fentanyl trade with little regard for the human toll. As these two powerful entities continue to operate with impunity, the international community faces an escalating crisis, with overdose deaths in the U.S. and beyond reaching record levels. The relationship between China and Mexico in this illicit enterprise is emblematic of a broader failure of global governance, where state actors either cannot or will not take decisive action against criminal networks for reasons of political convenience, economic benefit, or systemic corruption.

In the coming years, the challenge of dismantling this complex web of fentanyl trafficking will require unprecedented international cooperation, stronger regulatory frameworks, and a concerted effort to tackle the root causes of corruption and state complicity. Failing to address these issues will only perpetuate the cycle of addiction and death that fentanyl continues to unleash across the world.

Chapter 7: The Southern U.S. Border: A Weak Link in the Fight Against Fentanyl

The southern U.S. border has become a critical battleground in the fight against fentanyl, a synthetic opioid responsible for a surge in overdose deaths across the United States. As the drug continues to devastate communities, questions surrounding border security and the ability of U.S. law enforcement agencies to combat its influx have intensified. This chapter delves into how a combination of weakened border security policies and evolving smuggling tactics by Mexican cartels have facilitated the flow of fentanyl into the United States, and how transnational criminal organizations (TCOs) are exploiting these vulnerabilities. Moreover, the challenge of combating these operations is compounded by concerns of terrorism, as U.S. authorities struggle to manage the complexities of illegal immigration alongside the growing drug crisis.

The ease with which fentanyl can be synthesized and transported has made it an attractive commodity for drug cartels, particularly Mexican organizations that have taken over its production in recent years. What distinguishes fentanyl from other narcotics is not only its potency but also the sheer volume of it being smuggled across the southern U.S. border.

The Southern Border: A Porous Gateway

Stretching 2,000 miles, the southern U.S. border has long been a focal point for discussions about national security, immigration, and drug trafficking. While efforts to secure the border have intensified over the years, including physical barriers and increased personnel, the challenge remains significant. The geography of the region—ranging from urban ports of entry to vast, desolate deserts—presents logistical challenges for law enforcement agencies. In recent years, political shifts and fluctuating policies on border security have further weakened the border's defence, making it easier for fentanyl-laden shipments to slip through.

Weak points along the border are frequently exploited by Mexican cartels, who have become adept at finding and creating new routes for smuggling drugs. Whether through hidden compartments in commercial vehicles or employing "mules" individuals who carry drugs across the border the scale of these operations is staggering. According to U.S. Customs and Border Protection (CBP), seizures of fentanyl have skyrocketed in recent years, but this represents only a fraction of what is believed to be entering the country undetected.

Exploitation by Mexican Cartels

Mexican cartels, particularly the Sinaloa and Jalisco New Generation cartels, have established themselves as the dominant players in the fentanyl trade. Their operations extend beyond drug trafficking; these cartels have evolved into sophisticated, multinational enterprises capable of producing and distributing massive quantities of fentanyl. With laboratories on the Mexican side of the border, they rely on precursor chemicals imported from China to manufacture the drug in bulk. Once produced, the fentanyl is transported northward, destined for U.S. markets.

Cartels exploit the border's physical vulnerabilities but also take advantage of institutional and legal gaps. Cartel operatives are aware of the CBP's limited resources, which are often spread thin by a multitude of responsibilities, including combating human trafficking, processing migrants, and inspecting legal cargo. Cartels adapt quickly to enforcement strategies, using tactics such as creating false distractions to divert attention away from their primary smuggling routes. This may involve overwhelming a particular checkpoint with a surge of illegal migrants while drugs are funnelled through less-guarded areas.

The use of tunnel systems, some of which span from Tijuana to San Diego, is another tactic employed by cartels. These tunnels are often equipped with lighting, ventilation, and even rail systems, making them efficient conduits for drug smuggling. CBP and the Drug Enforcement Administration (DEA) have uncovered and shut down numerous tunnels, but the discovery of a single tunnel often represents the tip of a larger, more sophisticated network.

U.S. Customs and Border Protection: A Strained Frontline

The primary responsibility for protecting the U.S. southern border falls to CBP, a massive agency tasked with enforcing a wide range of immigration and trade laws. However, in the fight against fentanyl, the agency faces overwhelming challenges. The sheer volume of traffic across the border both legal and illegal makes it impossible to inspect every shipment or vehicle. The CBP's ability to conduct thorough inspections is further hampered by the need to process thousands of asylum seekers and other migrants, many of whom are fleeing violence and instability in their home countries.

The shifting political landscape has also affected the agency's ability to enforce border security. Policy changes related to immigration, the construction of physical barriers, and the allocation of resources have created uncertainty within the ranks of CBP. The agency must walk a fine line between upholding its mission of border security and navigating the often-contentious political debates surrounding immigration and law enforcement.

Despite these challenges, CBP has made significant strides in the detection and seizure of fentanyl shipments. The agency has invested in advanced technologies such as X-ray machines, drug-sniffing dogs, and chemical analysis tools. These tools allow officers to identify concealed drugs in vehicles, packages, and even within the human body. However, the ability to detect fentanyl, which is often hidden in minute quantities, remains a challenge due to its potency and the ingenuity of smugglers.

Evolving Smuggling Tactics and Countermeasures

The battle between U.S. law enforcement agencies and the cartels is one of adaptation. As CBP and other agencies develop innovative technologies and strategies, smugglers evolve their methods to counteract enforcement efforts. Smuggling fentanyl is not just a matter of moving enormous quantities of the drug across the border; cartels have become adept at micro-distribution, wherein fentanyl is smuggled in small, but highly potent amounts, often disguised within legal cargo or smuggled directly by individuals.

One common tactic is "blending," where smugglers hide fentanyl within legitimate goods, making it harder to detect without advanced scanning equipment. Similarly, the increasing use of drones to carry lesser amounts of drugs over the border is an innovation that has posed challenges for CBP. While drones can only carry limited quantities, they are difficult to track and can be deployed quickly across remote areas of the border.

In response, the U.S. government has taken steps to bolster its defence against these evolving threats. One of the most promising strategies is the increased cooperation between U.S. and Mexican authorities, as well as other international partners such as China, where many of the precursor chemicals for fentanyl are produced. Through intelligence-sharing and joint operations, these partnerships aim to dismantle the supply chains and distribution networks that fuel the fentanyl trade.

The Hidden Threat: Terrorism and the Southern Border

While the flow of fentanyl into the U.S. has captured much of the public's attention, there is another, less visible threat looming at the southern border: terrorism. In recent years, concerns have grown that the same smuggling routes used by Mexican cartels to traffic drugs could be exploited by terrorist organizations seeking to infiltrate the United States.

The fear is not unfounded. Transnational smuggling operations are notoriously difficult to monitor, and the considerable number of illegal border crossings each year presents a significant security challenge. While most migrants crossing the southern border are seeking a better life, law enforcement agencies must remain vigilant for those who may pose a threat to national security. The possibility of terrorist groups hiding amongst the waves of illegal migrants, using the same routes and tactics as drug smugglers, is a chilling prospect.

CBP, along with other federal agencies, has increased its focus on identifying and intercepting individuals with known ties to terrorist organizations. However, as with drug smuggling, the sheer scale of illegal crossings makes this task daunting. The presence of sophisticated cartels, who may not be ideologically aligned with terrorist groups but are motivated by profit, raises the spectre of cooperation between these two types of criminal enterprises. The concern is that cartels, in exchange for money or other resources, could facilitate the movement of terrorists across the border undetected.

Conclusion

The southern U.S. border is a complex and dynamic front in the war on drugs, particularly in the fight against fentanyl. As Mexican cartels continue to exploit weaknesses in border security, U.S. law enforcement agencies are in a constant race to keep up with the evolving tactics of these transnational criminal organizations. The fentanyl crisis has underscored the need for a more comprehensive approach to border security, one that balances the pressing need to stem the flow of dangerous drugs with the broader issues of immigration and national security.

The southern border remains a weak link in America's defence against not only the fentanyl epidemic but also potential terrorism. As U.S. authorities grapple with these dual threats, the need for stronger policies, better resources, and international cooperation has never been more urgent. Without a concerted effort to close these gaps, the devastating consequences of both fentanyl and other security risks will continue to ripple across the country, leaving lasting scars on communities and families alike.

Chapter 8: The Human Cost: Fentanyl's Devastation in the United States

Fentanyl, a synthetic opioid originally intended for pain management in cancer patients, has morphed into a drug of catastrophic proportions, driving an unprecedented public health crisis across the United States and Western Europe. Its extreme potency, affordability, and ease of production have made fentanyl the main driver of opioid-related deaths, and the growing crisis is testing the limits of law enforcement, public health systems, and political institutions. In this chapter, we explore the devastating human cost of fentanyl, the role of open-border policies in exacerbating the crisis, and the seeming inability or unwillingness of governments to stem the tide.

The Overdose Epidemic: A Spiraling Death Toll

Since the early 2010s, fentanyl has radically altered the landscape of drug abuse and overdose. In 2023, more than 100,000 Americans died from drug overdoses, with fentanyl involved in approximately two-thirds of these deaths. The introduction of fentanyl into the illicit drug market has thus accelerated a crisis that shows no signs of slowing down.

No region in the United States has been spared, and in recent years the crisis has spread to Western Europe, where fentanyl is becoming increasingly available. The impact is particularly severe in economically struggling areas, where substance abuse has long been intertwined with unemployment, poverty, and social instability. While the epidemic began in more impoverished, rural parts of the U.S., it has since engulfed urban and suburban areas as well.

Open Borders and the Role of Trafficking Networks

One of the most contentious aspects of the fentanyl crisis is the role that open-border policies in the U.S. and Europe have played in exacerbating the situation. The flow of fentanyl into the U.S. is often facilitated by transnational drug trafficking networks, particularly those based in Mexico, which receive precursor chemicals from China. Western Europe faces similar challenges, with fentanyl entering through various routes, often tied to organized crime networks that exploit porous borders.

Proponents of stricter immigration controls argue that the surge in drug trafficking is partly a by-product of weak border enforcement and lax immigration policies in recent years. Open-border policies, particularly in the U.S., have created new vulnerabilities for law enforcement, allowing cartels and traffickers easier access to markets where they can distribute fentanyl at an alarming rate. Border agencies, already overwhelmed by the surge in migration, struggle to stem the flow of illicit drugs amidst a chaotic and porous border environment.

Critics of current government policies argue that the political leadership has either ignored the crisis or is ideologically paralyzed, unable to adjust its stance on border control in the face of mounting evidence. Some see this as deliberate negligence, a refusal to admit the role of open-border policies in worsening the drug crisis. Others argue that the governments in power are ideologically committed to open borders for humanitarian or political reasons and are simply incapable of finding a balanced solution that both addresses human migration and curtails the flood of illicit drugs.

Disproportionate Impact on Marginalized Groups

The victims of this crisis span all demographic groups but marginalized and economically disadvantaged populations have borne the brunt of the devastation. Minority communities, particularly African

Americans and Latinos, have seen dramatic increases in fentanyl-related deaths. These groups, often already facing systemic barriers to healthcare and economic opportunity, are particularly vulnerable to the epidemic.

Homeless populations are especially at risk. As fentanyl's deadly reach extends through communities, those without stable housing find themselves not only susceptible to addiction but also more likely to encounter contaminated or laced drugs. Mental health disorders, already prevalent in disadvantaged populations, often lead to self-medication through opioids, creating a deadly feedback loop that many find impossible to escape.

Communities in Collapse: The Ripple Effect of Addiction

The impact of fentanyl addiction is not limited to those who directly suffer from addiction it radiates outward, tearing through families, destabilizing communities, and overwhelming local resources. Families are shattered by the loss of loved ones, and in some areas, entire neighbourhoods have been transformed into epicentres of despair. The children of addicted parents are often left orphaned, stretching already overburdened foster care systems to their breaking points.

The strain on public health systems is immense. Hospitals, already weakened by the COVID-19 pandemic, now struggle to cope with the flood of overdose cases. Emergency services, which rely heavily on naloxone (Narcan) to reverse overdoses, are experiencing burnout. Meanwhile, addiction services are underfunded, leaving many without access to critical treatment. In Europe, where healthcare systems are similarly stretched, the fentanyl crisis is beginning to put significant pressure on both social services and law enforcement, though it remains at an earlier stage than in the U.S.

Law Enforcement Overwhelmed: Rising Crime and Public Safety Concerns

Fentanyl's spread has resulted in a sharp uptick in crime, as addicts resort to theft and violence to sustain their drug habits. The explosion in drug-related criminal activity has overwhelmed law enforcement agencies, particularly in cities already grappling with surges in homelessness and poverty. Property crimes and violent crimes are on the rise as the economic fallout of addiction compounds the desperation felt by individuals caught in the grip of fentanyl.

The crisis has strained law enforcement's ability to respond effectively. In the U.S., local police forces are often the first responders to overdose cases and are increasingly reliant on Narcan to revive individuals who have overdosed. However, this short-term solution does little to address the root causes of addiction, and many of these individuals are caught in a cycle of repeated overdoses and resuscitation.

Compounding this challenge is the growing sophistication of drug trafficking networks. The international nature of fentanyl trafficking, particularly the production of precursors in China and the smuggling routes through Mexico has overwhelmed U.S. border control efforts. Many argue that current immigration policies have exacerbated this issue, as traffickers exploit the chaos of the border for their gain. Law enforcement officials have frequently cited the flood of illicit drugs through open borders as one of the most significant challenges they face in controlling the crisis.

The Political Stalemate: Governments Failing to Act

As the fentanyl crisis escalates, critics argue that the political leadership in both the U.S. and Western Europe has been either unwilling or unable to tackle the problem head-on. In the U.S., the debate over border security has become a partisan flashpoint, with opponents of stricter controls accusing the government of allowing the crisis to worsen by maintaining an open-border stance. Some suggest that the current administration's reluctance to tighten border controls is driven by ideological commitments, regardless of the human cost.

In Europe, governments face similar challenges. The fentanyl crisis is not yet as widespread as in the U.S., but there are growing concerns about the future, particularly as organized crime networks in Europe become more adept at exploiting weak immigration controls and legal loopholes.

Some argue that the political class is either ideologically incapable of addressing the crisis or too focused on other issues to give the drug epidemic the attention it demands.

Economic Consequences: A Nation Paying the Price

The economic cost of the fentanyl epidemic is astronomical, with public resources being diverted to cope with the drug's widespread devastation. The direct costs of healthcare, law enforcement, and incarceration are compounded by the indirect costs of lost productivity, unemployment, and the long-term care of children left orphaned by the crisis.

The criminalization of addiction has led to overcrowded prisons, particularly as law enforcement focuses on low-level offenders. Many of these individuals suffer from addiction but have little access to rehabilitation or mental health services in prison, perpetuating the cycle of drug abuse and criminality. Critics of this approach argue that it is not only economically unsustainable but morally flawed, failing to address the root causes of addiction.

Conclusion: A Crisis of Leadership, Policy, and Humanity

The fentanyl epidemic is not merely a public health crisis; it is a crisis of governance. The staggering human cost, measured in lives lost, communities destroyed, and economies weakened, is compounded by political inaction and ideological entrenchment. Open-border policies, while grounded in humanitarian ideals, have inadvertently allowed the crisis to grow, overwhelming law enforcement and enabling traffickers to exploit the vulnerabilities of modern immigration systems.

Addressing the fentanyl epidemic will require not only a shift in public health and law enforcement strategies but also a willingness on the part of governments to confront uncomfortable truths about the role of border control and immigration policies. Until policymakers acknowledge the interconnectedness of these issues, the fentanyl crisis will continue to devastate the lives of countless individuals and communities.

Chapter 9: Weaknesses in U.S. Law and Enforcement Responses

The United States faces an escalating public health and safety crisis as the opioid epidemic, particularly driven by fentanyl, claims more lives each year. Despite rising awareness and intense public outcry, U.S. law enforcement and legislative responses have struggled to effectively curb fentanyl trafficking. The reasons for this failure are complex, ranging from outdated laws to bureaucratic inefficiencies, as well as challenges rooted in both domestic and international law enforcement cooperation.

Outdated Laws and Policy Loopholes

The legal framework governing drug enforcement in the U.S. was established decades ago, primarily under the Controlled Substances Act of 1970. Although this legislation remains the backbone of federal drug policy, it has not kept pace with the rapidly changing landscape of synthetic drug trafficking. Fentanyl's potency, and the ease with which it can be modified chemically, present significant hurdles for law enforcement. Analogue laws designed to criminalize drugs that are like those already banned have proven insufficient, as traffickers stay one step ahead by tweaking chemical structures to circumvent these regulations. These loopholes have allowed synthetic opioids to flood the market while staying technically legal until the specific chemical variant is banned.

Even when specific fentanyl analogues are scheduled as controlled substances, enforcement becomes a matter of regulation playing catch-up with innovation. The legal process to classify a new analogue as a Schedule I drug can be slow, often requiring months or even years. This delay gives traffickers time to distribute vast quantities of new, unregulated analogues. Furthermore, small quantities of fentanyl can be lethal, making it difficult for law enforcement to handle seizures under existing guidelines. Possession laws, which often focus on weight-based thresholds, have not adapted to account for the extreme potency of fentanyl. For instance, an amount of fentanyl that could kill hundreds may not meet current threshold limits for more severe penalties under many state and federal guidelines.

Bureaucratic Inefficiencies and Agency Coordination

Drug enforcement in the U.S. is highly fragmented, involving numerous agencies with overlapping jurisdictions, including the Drug Enforcement Administration (DEA), Customs and Border Protection (CBP), Immigration and Customs Enforcement (ICE), and various state and local law enforcement entities. The DEA, tasked with leading the fight against fentanyl trafficking, faces challenges in coordinating efforts among these various bodies. These coordination gaps, exacerbated by bureaucracy and insufficient resource allocation, have undermined the efficacy of interdiction efforts. While federal agencies have the expertise and scope to address international aspects of fentanyl trafficking, local law enforcement often lacks the resources to deal with the street-level consequences, where fentanyl is mixed with other drugs like heroin or cocaine.

One key area where bureaucratic inefficiency stands out is in information-sharing across agencies. The siloed nature of U.S. law enforcement agencies often results in critical intelligence being delayed or lost. For example, border seizures of fentanyl-related materials may not immediately translate into actionable intelligence for DEA operations targeting domestic distribution networks. Similarly, international partnerships with countries that are key players in fentanyl production, like China or Mexico, are frequently stymied by diplomatic barriers and inconsistent cooperation.

The International Supply Chain: Complexities of Cross-Border Trafficking

Fentanyl production is a global issue, with most of the raw materials and finished products being manufactured overseas, primarily in China and Mexico. The complexity of tracking and dismantling international supply chains has proven difficult, particularly as transnational criminal organizations evolve their tactics.

As previously mentioned, China has historically been a significant source of precursor chemicals used to manufacture fentanyl, although recent efforts by the Chinese government to regulate these substances have forced many operations to move underground or relocate. Mexican drug cartels have capitalized on this shift, taking over sizable portions of the fentanyl production process. They obtain precursor chemicals from Chinese suppliers and then manufacture the finished product in clandestine labs before smuggling it across the U.S. southern border. This decentralized production model makes it difficult for U.S. law enforcement to target specific points in the supply chain.

Moreover, international cooperation in combatting fentanyl trafficking remains inconsistent. Diplomatic tensions with China have made it harder to establish formalized partnerships for tracking the flow of precursor chemicals. Although the U.S. and Mexico have collaborated on drug enforcement for decades, corruption within certain sectors of Mexican law enforcement and the sheer power of the cartels have hampered joint efforts to disrupt the fentanyl trade. These complications highlight the need for stronger, more consistent international cooperation, yet efforts are frequently mired in political and economic concerns that transcend the drug trade itself.

The Impact of Domestic Political Ideology on Law Enforcement

At the heart of the U.S. law enforcement response is the growing ideological rift over policing. In recent years, a vocal segment of political discourse, driven by progressive movements, has been increasingly critical of law enforcement agencies. This has inadvertently complicated efforts to address the fentanyl crisis. The ideological war on policing, particularly calls to defund or dismantle law enforcement agencies, has sapped both morale and resources from critical drug enforcement efforts.

In some cities, police departments have seen reductions in funding, leading to fewer officers on the streets and diminished capacity to engage in proactive policing strategies that could disrupt local drug distribution networks. This ideological battle has shifted attention away from supporting and modernizing law enforcement capabilities, focusing instead on reform measures that, while necessary in some cases, may be detracting from immediate public safety concerns like the opioid crisis.

The vilification of law enforcement, particularly by certain left-leaning factions, risks alienating the very agencies needed to combat the fentanyl epidemic. Public mistrust of the police, amplified by widespread social media campaigns, has led to a reluctance to cooperate between communities and law enforcement, further complicating local efforts to track and dismantle drug networks. While reforming and improving law enforcement practices should remain a goal, a nuanced approach is needed, one that balances reform with the recognition of law enforcement's vital role in addressing the fentanyl crisis.

Conclusion: A Multi-Pronged Strategy for Reform

To truly address the fentanyl epidemic, a multi-faceted strategy is needed, one that encompasses both domestic and international reform. First, U.S. lawmakers must modernize the legal framework surrounding synthetic drugs. This includes streamlining the process of banning new fentanyl analogues and revising possession laws to account for the potency of these substances. Additionally, addressing bureaucratic inefficiencies within U.S. law enforcement requires improving communication and cooperation between agencies. Enhanced information-sharing systems and more efficient use of resources could help to close the gaps currently exploited by traffickers.

On an international level, the U.S. must prioritize diplomatic and law enforcement cooperation with China, Mexico, and other countries involved in fentanyl production and distribution. Given the complexities of the supply chain, international partnerships will be critical in dismantling the networks responsible for trafficking fentanyl into the U.S.

Finally, the current ideological divide over policing must be addressed with care. While reform and accountability are important, vilifying law enforcement will only exacerbate the fentanyl crisis. A more balanced approach is needed—one that reforms policing where necessary but also empowers law enforcement agencies to confront the public health crisis that fentanyl presents.

Without significant changes to both the legal and enforcement frameworks, as well as a more nuanced political approach to law enforcement, fentanyl will continue to ravage American communities, claiming more lives each year.

Chapter 10: Reclassifying Fentanyl Trafficking as Murderous Intent

The opioid crisis in the United States has reached catastrophic levels, with fentanyl becoming a dominant factor in overdose deaths. Despite ongoing efforts to curb the spread of this lethal drug, current legal frameworks appear insufficient to address the gravity of its impact. Fentanyl is not merely an opioid; it is a synthetic drug with a potency so high that a few milligrams can cause death. When illicitly manufactured and distributed, it creates an epidemic of fatalities that far exceeds those caused by other narcotics. It is for this reason that we must radically rethink how fentanyl trafficking is prosecuted.

This chapter will argue for a dramatic shift in how we approach fentanyl-related crimes, proposing that the distribution of fentanyl be classified as an act of murderous intent. The idea of treating drug trafficking as murder may seem extreme but given the lethality of this substance and the knowledge traffickers have about its potency, it is time to reconsider the ethical and legal responsibilities of those involved in the trade. I will explore how current sentencing guidelines fall short of serving as effective deterrents and why redefining fentanyl trafficking as an act of murder could be a necessary and justifiable step to protect society.

The Unique Lethality of Fentanyl

It was originally developed for medical use to treat severe pain, particularly in cancer patients, but has since proliferated as a street drug. Unlike other opioids, which might lead to gradual addiction and eventual overdose, fentanyl can cause instant death in minute quantities. A dose as small as two milligrams, the size of a few grains of salt can be fatal. Given this knowledge, those who traffic fentanyl cannot claim ignorance about the consequences of their actions.

While other narcotics may be harmful, the immediate and often unintentional lethality of fentanyl places it in a different category altogether. Distributors of this drug know or should know, that they are disseminating death in powder form. This foreknowledge of the deadly potential of fentanyl forms the basis of the argument for reclassifying its distribution as an act of murderous intent.

The Shortcomings of Current Legal Frameworks

In the United States, fentanyl distribution is typically prosecuted under federal and state drug trafficking laws. These laws categorize trafficking as a serious crime, but the penalties often do not align with the severity of the harm inflicted. For example, federal mandatory minimum sentencing guidelines for drug offences, including fentanyl trafficking, may result in prison terms of five, 10, or 20 years depending on the quantity involved. However, these penalties are often based on the assumption that the harm caused by the drug is equivalent to that of other controlled substances like cocaine or heroin. This is a fundamental flaw in the law.

Fentanyl's unique lethality means that it should not be treated as just another dangerous narcotic. The existing legal penalties do not reflect the fact that fentanyl is routinely killing users, often without their knowledge that they are ingesting it. Many fentanyl-related deaths are the result of the drug being mixed into other narcotics like heroin or cocaine, or even counterfeit prescription pills, without the user's awareness. Current laws treat these deaths as tragic but unintended consequences of drug addiction, but this perspective ignores the deliberate actions of those who manufacture and distribute the drug.

Several case studies demonstrate how the leniency of current sentencing fails to provide justice for the victims of fentanyl overdoses. In one high-profile case, a dealer who distributed fentanyl-laced heroin that caused multiple deaths received a short prison sentence despite having prior knowledge that the drug mixture was lethal. In another case, a dealer was charged with manslaughter after selling fentanyl to an undercover officer, but the charge was reduced to drug trafficking in a plea deal. These cases highlight the insufficiency of existing legal mechanisms in addressing the deadly consequences of fentanyl distribution.

Reclassifying Fentanyl Trafficking as Murderous Intent

To address the disparity between the harm caused by fentanyl and the penalties meted out by current laws, we must consider reclassifying fentanyl trafficking as a crime with murderous intent. The reasoning here is not simply punitive but rooted in logic: anyone involved in the distribution of fentanyl is aware, or ought to be aware, of its deadly potential. By knowingly distributing a substance that is likely to kill, traffickers are engaging in conduct that can be interpreted as intentional, or at the very least, recklessly indifferent to human life.

To operationalize this shift, legislators could establish a legal framework where fentanyl trafficking which results in death is treated as second-degree murder or, in certain egregious cases, first-degree murder. This would place fentanyl distributors in a legal category closer to individuals who commit homicide, rather than mere drug dealers. It would also allow for harsher sentences, including life imprisonment without the possibility of parole, to be imposed on those who knowingly distribute this lethal substance.

This approach is not without precedent. In some U.S. states, "drug-induced homicide" laws have been enacted, where dealers can be charged with homicide if a customer dies because of ingesting drugs they supplied. These laws, however, are limited in scope and often face challenges in proving intent. By specifically focusing on fentanyl and framing its distribution as an act of murderous intent, the legal system could better reflect the unique threat posed by this drug.

Lessons from Other Jurisdictions: Canada, the UK, and Western Europe

The fentanyl crisis is not limited to the United States. Canada, the United Kingdom, and many Western European countries are also grappling with the rise of fentanyl-related deaths. In Canada, for example, the opioid epidemic has been declared a national public health emergency, and fentanyl is responsible for most overdose deaths. However, like the U.S., Canada has yet to adopt legal frameworks that treat fentanyl distribution as a crime of murderous intent.

In the UK and parts of Western Europe, fentanyl has not yet reached the same epidemic proportions, but there is growing concern about its potential spread. These countries could benefit from proactive legal measures that classify fentanyl trafficking as a homicidal act before the crisis escalates. By adopting harsher penalties for fentanyl distribution and treating deaths resulting from its use as murder, these nations could pre-empt the kind of devastation seen in North America.

Political and Social Obstacles

While the argument for reclassifying fentanyl trafficking as a crime of murderous intent is compelling from a legal and moral standpoint, the political and social feasibility of such a shift is far from certain. In the U.S., Canada, the UK, and Western Europe, many governments are currently led by left-leaning administrations that tend to prioritize rehabilitation and harm reduction over punitive measures. The idea of drastically increasing penalties for drug offences, particularly by introducing murder charges, may be seen as regressive or as a return to failed "War on Drugs" policies.

Additionally, there are concerns about racial and social justice. Drug laws in the U.S. have historically been disproportionately enforced against communities of colour, and there is a risk that harsher penalties for fentanyl trafficking could exacerbate these disparities. To address these concerns, any legal reforms should be carefully crafted to ensure equitable enforcement and to provide protections against excessive or unjust sentencing.

Nevertheless, the lethality of fentanyl demands bold action, and left-leaning governments must balance their commitment to harm reduction with the need to protect citizens from a substance that is killing thousands each year. The question is whether these governments have the political willpower to implement laws that would categorize fentanyl-related deaths as intentional acts of murder, even in the face of potential pushback from civil rights advocates.

Conclusion: A Call for Action

The fentanyl epidemic represents a unique and unprecedented challenge for legal systems around the world. It is a drug that does not merely harm; it kills, and it does so quickly and with terrifying efficiency. Current legal frameworks are ill-equipped to address the scale of the damage caused by fentanyl distribution. By reclassifying fentanyl trafficking as a crime of murderous intent, we can send a clear message that society will no longer tolerate the reckless spread of this deadly substance.

Tougher penalties, including the possibility of murder charges, may act as a much-needed deterrent for traffickers who currently face sentences that are insufficient given the deadly consequences of their actions. It is time for governments in the U.S., Canada, the UK, and Western Europe to confront the fentanyl crisis with the seriousness it demands, even if doing so requires a radical rethinking of how we prosecute drug-related crimes.

Chapter 11: Labeling Cartels as Terrorist Organizations

The designation of Mexican drug cartels as terrorist organizations is a matter that has gained significant traction in recent years, driven by the growing scale of destruction caused by their activities most notably the trafficking of fentanyl and the increasing instability in U.S.-Mexico relations. While previous chapters have explored the devastation caused by the fentanyl crisis, including the staggering death toll and the societal impacts on American communities, it is now crucial to focus on the more comprehensive and urgent argument for formally labelling these cartels as terrorist entities.

The current geopolitical context makes this discussion even more pressing. Relations between the United States and Mexico have become strained, as Mexico's actions under its current government reflect a lack of cooperation on key issues of mutual security. Beyond the drug trade, Mexico has allowed the unimpeded movement of illegal migrants through its territory, directly contributing to the crisis at the U.S. southern border. Moreover, the growing influence of China in Mexico particularly its substantial investments in critical sectors such as electric vehicle (EV) production poses a further challenge to U.S. interests in the region. This chapter will explore why the Mexican cartels' designation as terrorist organizations not only addresses the immediate threat posed by their criminal operations but also serves as a broader strategy to counter the destabilizing influences both within and beyond Mexico's borders.

The Case for Designation: Expanding the Definition of Terrorism

Traditional definitions of terrorism emphasize the use of violence and intimidation to pursue political, ideological, or religious objectives. However, the evolution of non-state actors has blurred these distinctions, particularly as criminal enterprises like the Mexican cartels operate with similar levels of organization, violence, and cross-border influence as recognized terrorist organizations.

The cartels, including infamous groups like the Sinaloa Cartel, Jalisco New Generation Cartel (CJNG), and others, exert control over vast swaths of Mexican territory through brutal violence, intimidation, and corruption. Their tactics of mass killings, beheadings, kidnappings, and attacks on law enforcement are not merely criminal but strategic. These actions serve to destabilize regions, deter government intervention, and maintain their dominance over drug trafficking routes, which include the lethal fentanyl pipeline to the United States. Though their motives are primarily financial, their violence and methods of control have a profound political impact, undermining both Mexico's governance and U.S. national security.

Furthermore, these cartels have adopted transnational operations, expanding their influence into the U.S. through extensive drug distribution networks and infiltrating American communities. The fentanyl epidemic is the most visible sign of their reach, but their operations also include human trafficking, arms smuggling, and money laundering, creating a sophisticated web of criminality that increasingly resembles the operational structures of terrorist organizations.

Given the extreme violence, global reach, and profound destabilization caused by these cartels, the time has come to recognize them as terrorist organizations. Designating them as such would reflect the reality of their threat, and it would provide the United States with a more robust framework to combat their operations.

Mexico's Role in Enabling Cartel Power

The Mexican government's role in managing, or enabling, the cartels' power cannot be overlooked. In recent years, Mexico's actions have strained relations with the United States. Under the administration of President Andrés Manuel López Obrador (AMLO), Mexico has adopted a "hugs, not bullets" approach to cartel violence, often refusing to confront these organizations head-on. This policy has allowed the cartels to flourish, with little fear of serious government crackdowns.

Moreover, Mexico has facilitated the flow of illegal migrants through its territory, allowing them to travel unimpeded to the U.S. southern border. In many cases, organized crime syndicates, including cartels, are directly involved in human smuggling operations, profiting from both migrant exploitation and the U.S. border crisis. This not only exacerbates the already tense immigration situation but also demonstrates Mexico's unwillingness to act as a partner in addressing security challenges that affect both nations.

Further complicating this dynamic is China's growing presence in Mexico. As China seeks to expand its influence in Latin America, it has begun investing heavily in Mexican industries, most notably the EV manufacturing sector. With billions of dollars flowing into Mexico's economy, China is securing critical relationships with Mexican officials and gaining leverage over the country's strategic direction. This influx of Chinese capital and influence presents a clear challenge to U.S. geopolitical interests in the region. If the United States cannot rely on Mexico as an ally in addressing the cartels, border security, or countering Chinese influence, it must rethink its strategy for ensuring regional stability.

The Chinese government's involvement in Mexican industries raises concerns not only about economic competition but also about security. China has a well-documented history of using its investments to influence government decisions and policies, often aligning with regimes that resist U.S. influence. If Mexico becomes increasingly aligned with Chinese interests, it could become even less cooperative with U.S.

security objectives, particularly in combatting the cartels and securing the border. Therefore, designating cartels as terrorist organizations could also serve as a signal to Mexico that the U.S. will take decisive action to protect its national interests, regardless of Mexican or Chinese interference.

Legal and Strategic Benefits of the Terrorist Designation

Designating Mexican cartels as terrorist organizations would have far-reaching legal and strategic benefits for the United States. Under the Foreign Terrorist Organization (FTO) framework, the U.S. would be able to enhance its legal authority to combat cartel operations more aggressively. The FTO designation expands the jurisdiction of federal agencies, such as the FBI, DEA, and Department of Homeland Security, enabling them to use counterterrorism statutes to target individuals and entities that provide material support to the cartels.

One of the key advantages of this designation is the ability to target the cartels' financial infrastructure more effectively. Like terrorist groups, cartels rely on sophisticated money-laundering networks to fund their operations. The FTO designation would allow the U.S. Treasury and financial institutions to freeze cartel assets, block financial transactions, and impose severe penalties on anyone involved in supporting these organizations. By cutting off their financial lifelines, the U.S. could significantly weaken the cartels' ability to operate.

Additionally, designating cartels as terrorist organizations would enhance international cooperation. The U.S. could work more closely with its allies to pressure Mexico to take more decisive action against the cartels. European and Latin American nations, many of whom are also affected by the global drug trade, would be more likely to align with U.S. counterterrorism efforts, providing additional resources and diplomatic pressure to curtail cartel influence. The designation would also make it easier for the U.S. to extradite cartel leaders and operatives from countries where they may seek refuge.

The Diplomatic Fallout: Risks and Rewards

While the legal and strategic benefits of designating cartels as terrorist organizations are substantial, the diplomatic fallout from such a decision must also be carefully considered. Mexico, already at odds with the U.S. on several fronts, would resist this designation vehemently. The Mexican government would see such a move as a direct challenge to its sovereignty and an implicit accusation of its failure to control its territory.

However, given Mexico's unwillingness to address the cartel problem effectively and its tacit cooperation with U.S. adversaries such as China, the U.S. must weigh the risks of diplomatic tension against the urgent need to protect its citizens. Labelling the cartels as terrorist organizations would be a clear message to both Mexico and China that the U.S. will not stand by while its national security is compromised by criminal organizations and foreign influence. It may also prompt Mexico to reconsider its position, especially if U.S. economic and security aid is made contingent on more active cooperation.

A Necessary Shift in Policy

The time has come for the U.S. to recognize the full scale of the threat posed by Mexican drug cartels. These organizations have evolved beyond mere criminal enterprises; they are powerful, violent, transnational organizations whose operations directly harm American citizens and undermine U.S. national security. Their partnership with Chinese manufacturers, their role in human trafficking, and their complicity in the fentanyl crisis make them a clear and present danger.

Labelling Mexican cartels as terrorist organizations is not just a legal manoeuvre; it is a strategic imperative. The cartels must be treated with the same seriousness as any other terrorist threat to the United States. While the diplomatic and political consequences of such a designation will be complex, the U.S. cannot afford to allow these organizations to continue operating unchecked. The future stability of the region, the integrity of U.S. borders, and the safety of American citizens demand decisive action.

Conclusion

Designating Mexican cartels as terrorist organizations represents a necessary escalation in the fight against an unprecedented threat. It reflects the reality that the cartels, in their violence, corruption, and cross-border influence, mirror the operations of globally recognized terrorist groups. With strained relations between the U.S. and Mexico, and the growing involvement of China in Mexican affairs, the stakes have never been higher. This designation would allow the U.S. to mobilize all necessary resources to disrupt cartel operations and safeguard national security interests in an increasingly hostile regional environment.

Chapter 12: Future Strategies for Combating the Fentanyl Crisis

The fentanyl crisis remains one of the most insidious public health challenges of our time. While previous chapters have explored the devastating effects of fentanyl on individuals, families, and communities, it is now critical to examine the systemic factors that have allowed this crisis to persist and, in some cases, flourish. Among these factors is the role of China, a country that, while working to combat the flow of fentanyl, appears to be doing little more than giving lip service to the issue. In a nation known for its highly controlled, authoritarian regime, the idea that illegal fentanyl production and export could thrive without the Chinese government's tacit approval is difficult to accept.

Furthermore, the overwhelming impact of the fentanyl crisis is compounded by broader issues in the United States, including a broken immigration system that has strained public resources—particularly in healthcare. Millions of illegal immigrants, many of whom lack access to basic health services, are taxing an already overwhelmed system. These challenges are not isolated but interconnected, and any effective strategy to combat the fentanyl crisis must acknowledge both the global and domestic forces that perpetuate it.

China's Role: Lip Service and Lax Enforcement

While China has publicly pledged to combat the production and export of fentanyl, the reality on the ground suggests otherwise. China remains the largest source of fentanyl precursor chemical compounds used to synthesize the drug and despite regulations that ban the production and export of fentanyl, these chemicals continue to flow out of China with alarming ease. The question is not whether China can stop this; it is whether China is truly motivated to do so.

A Controlled State with Uncontrolled Trafficking

China is one of the most tightly controlled nations in the world, with an extensive surveillance apparatus, strict government oversight of the economy, and a police state that can swiftly quell dissent. Given this, it is implausible to suggest that the Chinese government is unaware of the extensive production of fentanyl precursors within its borders. If the Chinese government genuinely wanted to halt the flow of these chemicals, it has both the tools and the infrastructure to do so. Yet, production continues, and the global fentanyl trade thrives. This raises troubling questions about China's complicity in allowing the trade to persist, whether for economic, geopolitical, or other undisclosed reasons.

Token Measures: A Diplomatic Façade

In recent years, China has taken some actions to address international pressure, such as formally scheduling fentanyl and related substances as controlled substances. However, these measures seem to be more about managing international relations than stopping the problem at its source. Regulatory loopholes and a lack of enforcement suggest that these efforts are performative. Chinese chemical companies can skirt regulations by slightly altering the molecular structure of fentanyl precursors, thus avoiding scrutiny. Furthermore, enforcement of these regulations is often lax, with local officials either turning a blind eye or being actively complicit in the trade.

Re-examining U.S.-China Relations in the Context of Fentanyl

Given China's apparent unwillingness to take substantive action, the United States must rethink its approach to U.S.-China relations concerning the fentanyl crisis. Diplomatic overtures have failed to yield meaningful results, and a more hardline approach may be necessary. If the Chinese government is unwilling to take responsibility for its role in the global fentanyl trade, then the United States must seek alternative avenues to pressure China into compliance.

Economic Sanctions and Trade Penalties

One approach is the imposition of targeted economic sanctions on Chinese companies and officials who are directly or indirectly involved in the production and export of fentanyl precursors. These sanctions would serve as both a punitive measure and a deterrent, signalling that the United States will no longer tolerate China's passive complicity. Trade penalties could also be leveraged against industries that benefit from fentanyl production, applying economic pressure on China to enforce its laws and regulations more stringently.

Leveraging International Partnerships

In addition to direct actions against China, the U.S. should work with its international allies to form a coalition aimed at addressing the fentanyl crisis. A united front, with multiple nations demanding greater accountability from China, would carry more diplomatic weight than isolated efforts. Furthermore, this coalition could work to cut off other supply routes and sources of precursors in countries like India, which has also played a growing role in the global fentanyl trade.

Border Security and Domestic Challenges

Even as international efforts are made to curtail the flow of fentanyl, the United States must address the crisis at home. Fentanyl continues to enter the country primarily through the southern border, and the U.S. border security apparatus has struggled to keep pace with traffickers. However, the issue is compounded by another growing concern: the influx of millions of illegal immigrants, many of whom are straining the U.S. healthcare system.

An Overwhelmed Healthcare System

The fentanyl crisis does not exist in isolation. America's healthcare system is buckling under the weight of millions of people who have crossed into the country illegally and who often lack access to paid health services. Hospitals in border states are facing a dual crisis: an influx of opioid overdose cases due to fentanyl and a population explosion of undocumented immigrants who require medical attention but often lack the means to pay for it. This overwhelming demand is siphoning resources away from addiction treatment and prevention services that could otherwise be directed toward U.S. citizens and legal residents suffering from opioid addiction.

Securing the Border: A National Imperative

To combat both the fentanyl crisis and the strain on public resources, it is imperative to bolster border security. Current efforts have proven insufficient in halting the flow of fentanyl, which is often smuggled in small quantities that evade detection. Upgrading technology at ports of entry, such as implementing more sensitive drug-detection devices and investing in advanced scanning systems, will be critical in preventing fentanyl from crossing the border. Additionally, improving intelligence sharing between U.S. law enforcement agencies and their Mexican counterparts could lead to more effective interdiction efforts.

Improving Drug Enforcement Tactics

Beyond border security, U.S. drug enforcement agencies must adapt to the ever-changing tactics of fentanyl traffickers. Traditional methods of interdiction are becoming less effective in the face of more sophisticated trafficking networks, many of which operate through online platforms and encrypted communications.

Cyber Enforcement and Digital Monitoring

The rise of the dark web and other online marketplaces has made it easier for traffickers to sell fentanyl with relative anonymity. Law enforcement must continue to enhance its cyber capabilities, developing specialized task forces focused on disrupting online drug sales. In addition, public and private sector collaboration could be expanded to monitor the financial transactions that fund these illicit networks.

Expanding Public Health Measures

While securing borders and enforcing drug laws is crucial, it is not enough to address the public health catastrophe caused by fentanyl.

Addiction treatment services, already strained, are further burdened by the influx of illegal immigrants who also require medical care. The costs of treatment for opioid addiction are significant, and many healthcare providers are struggling to keep pace.

Investment in Addiction Treatment and Harm Reduction

Expanding access to medication-assisted treatment (MAT) and other addiction services must remain a priority, despite the strain on resources. One approach is to divert more federal funding toward community-based treatment programs, focusing on areas hardest hit by fentanyl. Harm reduction strategies, such as the availability of naloxone and fentanyl test strips, should also be expanded to reduce overdose deaths. However, these efforts must be matched by stronger immigration enforcement and reform to prevent illegal immigrants from further overwhelming the system.

Education and Technological Advancements

A long-term solution to the fentanyl crisis will require a significant investment in education and technological advancements. Public awareness campaigns that inform individuals of the dangers of fentanyl and provide resources for addiction treatment are essential. Moreover, the development of new detection technologies, such as portable chemical analyzers and AI-driven drug trafficking detection systems, will be key to staying ahead of traffickers.

Conclusion

In conclusion, the fentanyl crisis is a complex, multifaceted issue that requires both international and domestic solutions. China's role in the production and export of fentanyl precursors cannot be ignored, and the United States must take a firmer stance in demanding accountability from the Chinese government. At the same time, the U.S. must address the dual challenge of illegal immigration and an overwhelmed healthcare system, which are compounding the strain on addiction treatment resources. A holistic approach—one that includes stronger border security, improved drug enforcement tactics, expanded public health measures, and cutting-edge technological advancements—will be necessary to combat the fentanyl crisis effectively. Only through sustained, coordinated efforts can we hope to turn the tide on this deadly epidemic.

Chapter 13: The Endgame – The Looming Shadow of Open Conflict

As we conclude our exploration of China's hybrid warfare against the West through the lens of fentanyl, the question arises: What is the goal of Beijing's strategy, and what might the future hold? This is not simply a war of attrition, fought through the weaponization of synthetic opioids; it is part of a broader, more complex campaign designed to weaken Western nations economically, socially, and militarily. As China's influence grows through economic initiatives like the Belt and Road, and its geopolitical alliances with powers such as Russia, Iran, and North Korea solidify, the possibility of a larger, more conventional conflict cannot be ignored.

The United States, and the West in general, finds itself at a critical juncture. Experts warn that Washington is ill-prepared for an open confrontation with Beijing, let alone the prospect of a multi-front war against a coalition of adversaries that includes China, Russia, Iran, and North Korea. The alarming decrease in U.S. defence spending, which now accounts for just 3% of GDP compared to 17% at the height of the Cold War suggests a troubling lack of readiness. While the West is engaged in this slow-burning conflict of hybrid warfare, its adversaries have been quietly preparing for the next phase.

China's Belt and Road Initiative, launched in 2013, is a masterstroke of global strategy. Through this program, Beijing has invested in critical infrastructure across Asia, Africa, and Europe, creating economic dependencies that enhance its geopolitical influence. But more than that,

China has taken control of vast resources, particularly in the realm of critical minerals. These minerals, which are essential for everything from advanced weapon systems to consumer electronics, position China as a gatekeeper in the global supply chain. The West, especially the U.S., is now vulnerable not just in terms of economic dependence on Chinese goods, but also in its capacity to sustain a prolonged military conflict.

This raises a troubling question: Has China positioned itself for an endgame that involves more than just weakening the West through drugs, economic influence, and technological superiority? Is the goal a form of confrontation, in which the West finds itself too divided, too under-resourced, and too politically fractured to mount an effective defence? If so, the fentanyl crisis may only be the beginning of China's grander strategy of global supremacy.

For decades, the U.S. and its allies have enjoyed the security of military dominance. But that dominance is being eroded, not just by budget cuts, but by the lack of attention to the emerging threats posed by adversaries who have spent the last two decades preparing for conflict on multiple fronts. While the West has been mired in conflicts in the Middle East, China has been methodically building its military, technological, and economic capabilities. It has done so with a clear understanding that modern warfare is as much about controlling resources, technology, and global supply chains as it is about military strength.

The U.S. military, once unrivalled, now faces the sobering reality of obsolescence in key areas. China has made significant strides in artificial intelligence, quantum computing, and missile technology, while also building a formidable navy capable of challenging U.S. dominance in the Pacific. Meanwhile, Russia, Iran, and North Korea continue to pose significant threats each of them capable of opening new fronts in a conflict that could stretch Western military resources to their breaking point. The West is facing a potential scenario where it must confront not just one, but multiple adversaries, each with the capability to exploit specific weaknesses.

The fentanyl crisis, when viewed in this broader context, seems less like a tragic epidemic and more like a symptom of a much larger, multi-dimensional campaign aimed at eroding the West's strength and resolve. China's long-term strategy is not just about winning battles; it is about creating a world order in which the West is no longer the dominant force. By weakening the U.S. economically, socially, and militarily, China positions itself as the unchallenged global power.

But this raises a critical question for policymakers in Washington, London, Paris, and other Western capitals: How can the West prepare itself for this new reality? Can the United States, with its current level of defence spending and divided political landscape, effectively counter a multi-front war involving adversaries as diverse as China, Russia, Iran, and North Korea? The uncomfortable truth is that without significant changes in both strategy and resources, the answer may be no.

To meet this challenge, the West must first recognize the interconnected nature of modern warfare. Hybrid warfare is not confined to any single arena whether it be economics, technology, or military strength. It spans all of these, and to successfully counter China's ambitions, the West must strengthen its defences across all fronts. This includes restoring defence spending to levels that reflect the growing global threats, but it also means addressing the vulnerabilities that have emerged in other areas most notably, the reliance on Chinese-controlled resources and technologies.

Moreover, Western nations must unite in their response. China's strategy thrives on division—whether it be economic dependencies through the Belt and Road Initiative, or social discord fueled by drug addiction and economic inequality. To counter this, the West must present a unified front, not just in military terms, but also in its economic policies, technological innovations, and societal resilience.

The ultimate endgame remains unclear. China does not seek direct military confrontation, but rather a gradual, strategic weakening of the West until it can impose its will without the need for open conflict. However, the possibility of miscalculation where a series of smaller conflicts or crises spiral into a broader war cannot be dismissed. If the West continues to neglect its defences, both military and economic, it risks being caught off guard, facing an adversary that has spent decades preparing for this very moment.

The fentanyl crisis is just one part of this broader strategy, but it serves as a potent reminder of how modern warfare is evolving. The West must adapt to this new reality, or risk being outmanoeuvred by adversaries who have long understood that the future of war is as much about controlling resources, information, and technology as it is about traditional military strength.

As we move forward, the question remains: Will the West recognize the true nature of this conflict, or will it remain reactive, only responding once the damage has been done? The answer to that question may well determine the future of global power and the fate of the world as we know it.

Epilogue: A War Yet to End

As the concluding chapter in this book closes, the story of fentanyl's deadly impact on the United States remains unfinished. The statistics tell a grim tale thousands of lives lost, countless families shattered, and entire communities plunged into despair. Yet, what has become clear throughout these pages is that this crisis is not just a matter of addiction or poor border control. It is a deeply embedded component of a larger geopolitical struggle, one that stretches beyond the opioid epidemic and into the realm of hybrid warfare.

China, a nation long experienced in the art of strategy and indirect confrontation, has evolved its methods of undermining adversaries. The same philosophies that guided Chinese military thinking in the era of the Warring States have found new expression in modern-day tactics, including economic manipulation, technological supremacy, and, disturbingly, the weaponization of drugs. Fentanyl, with its lethal potency and ease of manufacture, has become a tool in this modern form of warfare. Unlike the Opium Wars of the 19th century, where China was once the victim of Western narcotic exploitation, the tables have turned. Today, it is the West, particularly the United States, which finds itself caught in a web of addiction and societal destabilization.

Through its complex networks of fentanyl precursor production, state-sponsored pharmaceutical companies, and strategic partnerships with Mexican cartels, China has managed to inflict severe damage on the U.S. without firing a single shot. As this book has detailed, the Southern U.S. border has become a conduit for a synthetic poison that flows from the factories of China to the streets of America, with catastrophic results. Meanwhile, the Mexican cartels, operating with impunity, act as both collaborators and enablers, smuggling fentanyl across the border and deep into American communities.

The failure to recognize the full scope of this crisis has resulted in a patchwork of responses piecemeal law enforcement efforts, limited international cooperation, and a lack of meaningful accountability for the true architects of this devastation. The legal and political systems in the United States have proven ill-equipped to handle the scale of this modern hybrid threat, as existing laws fail to address the unique lethality of fentanyl and the global nature of its distribution. This book has argued for radical rethinking in how we prosecute fentanyl traffickers, how we categorize Mexican cartels, and how we address the role of China in fueling this crisis.

Yet, even as we look forward, we must acknowledge that the solutions proposed within these pages will face considerable resistance. Redefining fentanyl distribution as an act of murderous intent and designating Mexican cartels as terrorist organizations would require significant political will and unprecedented cooperation at the international level. These steps may also invite fierce retaliation from both the cartels and China itself, adding complexity to an already delicate geopolitical landscape. Nonetheless, bold actions are required by the U.S. to regain control over its borders, protect its citizens, and restore its societal stability.

The future of this war against fentanyl will not be won through enforcement alone. It must be complemented by a comprehensive strategy that addresses the deeper issues at play: the porous borders, the supply chains linking Chinese manufacturers to Mexican traffickers, and the socio-economic conditions that make communities vulnerable to addiction. Moreover, the fight against fentanyl must be understood not just as a matter of public health or crime, but as a broader national security threat. Only when we recognize the strategic intent behind this crisis can we begin to mount an effective defence.

As readers, policymakers, and citizens, it is incumbent upon us to recognize the ongoing nature of this battle. The death toll from fentanyl is not merely a tragic by-product of the global drug trade it is the visible wound of a larger, more insidious conflict. A conflict that is far from over.

The war on fentanyl is part of a wider, hybrid war being waged against the United States. A war of attrition, fought not with armies, but with chemicals and networks. It is a war that has left no American community untouched, and yet it remains misunderstood.

If there is one message to take from this book, it is that the fight against fentanyl cannot be fought in isolation. It is part of a larger struggle one that requires not only stronger laws and better enforcement but also an awareness of the geopolitical forces at work. This is a war that demands vigilance, unity, and most importantly, the will to confront the threats posed by those who seek to weaken the United States from within.

The crisis is not over, but the battle lines have been drawn. What remains to be seen is how the United States will respond.

Will it rise to the challenge, or will it allow this silent war to continue claiming its victims unchecked?

The answer lies in what we do next.

John Shenton

End

Did you love *Silent Weapon*? Then you should read *The Dragon's Gambit: China's Bid for Global Dominance and the Western Response*[1] by John Shenton!

[2]

In the 21st century, few challenges loom as large on the global stage as the rapid rise of China, and it's bid to assert dominance in every sphere of international influence. The Dragon's Gambit: China's Bid for Global Dominance and the Western Response provides a detailed, multifaceted exploration of this phenomenon, offering readers a critical examination of China's strategic ambitions and the global repercussions. This book does more than recount history—it dissects China's current manoeuvres, scrutinizing the far-reaching consequences and posing urgent questions for the West's response.

---

1. https://books2read.com/u/bzyZ9E

2. https://books2read.com/u/bzyZ9E

Also by John Shenton

Business Plan Basics
The Bahamas - More Islands and Recipes Than You Expect!
Collected Musings from Bricks and Mortar to E-commerce
The Smart City Odyssey: Unveiling the Secrets to Traveller-Centric
Software
The Dragon's Gambit: China's Bid for Global Dominance and the
Western Response
Silent Weapon
Business Basics: Money Sources
Influx
Fried Chips
Mandates, Motors, and Misinformation
Echos of Orwell
Control and Chaos
The Empire's Warning: What Rome's Fall Tells Us About the West
Today

About the Author

John Shenton was born in Birmingham, England and grew up in postwar England. He spent several years as a Radio Officer onboard a variety of vessels sailing to the Persian Gulf, the Indian Ocean and South China seas.

With degrees and a background in electronics and computers he has lived and worked within the United Kingdom, Germany, Switzerland and Canada.

While doing so, he established numerous trading relationships in Japan, Korea, the USA, China and other countries.

He has been retired for some time now living in Montréal Canada enjoying golfing, writing, sailing and many other things automotive.

About the Publisher

John Shenton published via Draft2digital